ECV146-Life in the Roman Empire (eBook)

Cavendish Square 4 Volumes Flipbook
Set Price: $213.84
Reading Level:6th Grade
Interest Level: Middle
Accelerated Reader: No

From patricians to slaves, Life in the Roman Empire explores the daily lives of the ancient Romans. Each book in the series provides insight into Rome's hierarchical society. The series also details the infrastructure that supported the empire, including the ways that those living in cities and towns contributed to its success. Life in the Roman Empire presents a comprehensive view of ancient Rome at its peak.

Title	Code	List Price	Our Price	Copyright	Pro
Patricians in the Roman Empire	ECV622587	$71.28	$53.46	2017	
Religion in the Roman Empire	ECV622648	$71.28	$53.46	2017	
The City in the Roman Empire	ECV622600	$71.28	$53.46	2017	
The Countryside in the Roman Empire	ECV622624	$71.28	$53.46	2017	

LIFE IN THE ROMAN EMPIRE

THE CITY IN THE ROMAN EMPIRE

DANIEL MACKLEY

Cavendish
Square

New York

Library of Congress Cataloging-in-Publication Data

Names: Mackley, Daniel, author.
Title: The city in the Roman Empire / Daniel Mackley.
Description: New York : Cavendish Square Publishing, [2017] | Series: Life in the Roman Empire |
Includes bibliographical references and index. |
Description based on print version record and CIP data provided by publisher; resource not viewed.
Identifiers: LCCN 2016032150 (print) | LCCN 2016023651 (ebook) |
ISBN 9781502622594 (library bound) | ISBN 9781502622600 (ebook)
Subjects: LCSH: Cities and towns--Rome--History--Juvenile literature. |
City and town life--Rome--History--Juvenile literature. | Rome--Social conditions--Juvenile literature. |
Rome--Social life and customs--Juvenile literature. |
Rome--History--Empire, 30 B.C.-476 A.D.--Juvenile literature.
Classification: LCC HT114 (print) | LCC HT114 .M33 2017 (ebook) |
DDC 307.7609456/32--dc23
LC record available at https://lccn.loc.gov/2016032150

Editorial Director: David McNamara
Editor: Caitlyn Miller
Copy Editor: Nathan Heidelberger
Associate Art Director: Amy Greenan
Designer: Joseph Macri
Production Coordinator: Karol Szymczuk
Photo Research: J8 Media

The photographs in this book are used by permission and through the courtesy of: Cover Sergey Borisov/Alamy; p. 4, 6, 19, 62 DEA PICTURE LIBRARY/De Agostini Picture Library/Getty Images; p. 14 Galerie Daniel Greiner, Paris, France/ Archives Charmet/Bridgeman Images; p. 24 duncan1890/E+/Getty Images; p. 26 ©North Wind Picture Archives; p. 30 Luxerendering/Shutterstock.com; p. 32 De Agostini Picture Library/G. Dagli Orti/Bridgeman Images; p. 36 Ancient Art and Architecture Collection Ltd./Bridgeman Images; p. 39 Brooklyn Museum of Art, New York, USA/Bridgeman Images; p. 40 Delaware Art Museum, Wilmington, USA/F.V. DuPont Acquisition Fund/Bridgeman Images; p. 40 Marie-Lan Nguyen/ Wikimedia Commons/File:Bronze young girl reading CdM Paris.jpg; p. 46 MatthiasKabel assumed/Wikimedia Commons/ File:Roman statue of girl playing astragaloi 14 aC.jpg; p. 49 Giakita/Alamy; p. 51 De Agostini Picture Library/S. Vannini/ Bridgeman Images; p. 54 National Geographic Creative/Bridgeman Images; p. 56 J. Paul Getty Museum, Los Angeles, USA/ Bridgeman Images; p. 59 Philip and Elizabeth De Bay/Corbis Historical/Getty Images; p. 65 Musee des Beaux-Arts Andre Malraux, Le Havre, France/Bridgeman Images; p. 67 Lautz/Shutterstock.com; p. 69 Mauricio Abreu/AWL Images/ Getty Images.

Printed in the United States of America

Contents

The Foundations of the Roman Empire

At its peak, Rome ruled nearly 4 percent of the land on Earth.

The entirety of a sweeping empire, one that ultimately stretched from Britain to Persia, began with a single city: Rome. While the majority of citizens in ancient Rome lived out their days in the countryside, it is still the **Forum** we think of when we reflect on life in ancient Rome. The city of Rome was a vibrant place that served as the empire's seat of power, and the Forum was a public gathering space where deals were struck, goods sold, and ideas exchanged.

The city itself was founded in 753 BCE. Legend says that two twin brothers, Romulus and Remus, vied for power. When Romulus emerged as the victor, he named the city after himself. This single city quickly transformed into an empire. Once ruled by kings, the Roman Empire shifted to become a republic after the overthrow of Tarquin the Proud in 509 BCE. Then, in 27 BCE, Augustus became the first emperor of Rome. Emperors would command Europe until 476 CE, when the empire lost its control of the continent at the hands of barbarians (the Romans' term for anyone outside of Rome).

In this book, you will learn about craftsmen, merchants, slaves, soldiers, and other residents of Roman cities from 27 BCE to 200 CE, the first two centuries of the empire. The urban lifestyle of ancient Rome looks quite different from city life today. Picture public baths and over-the-top spectacles. Picture banquets and day-to-day chores. This was life in the city in ancient Rome.

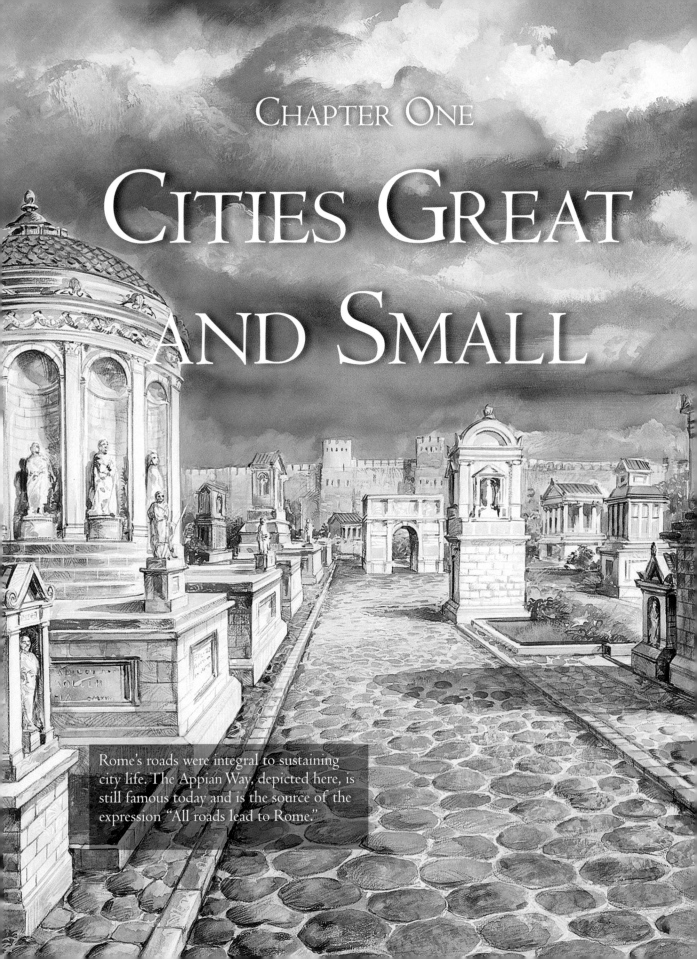

CHAPTER ONE
CITIES GREAT AND SMALL

Rome's roads were integral to sustaining city life. The Appian Way, depicted here, is still famous today and is the source of the expression "All roads lead to Rome."

Livy (59 or 64 BCE–17 CE) was a Roman historian who wrote a sweeping history of the whole of the empire across 142 books. In these volumes, Livy also traces the city of Rome's development from a rudimentary patch of land to a sophisticated metropolis, which was home to around one million people at its height.

Rome was the capital of the empire. The next largest cities in the empire were Alexandria (Egypt) and Carthage (in what is now Tunisia), each with a population of some five hundred thousand. In other words, the population of the next largest cities were the size of just the slave population in the city of Rome. Yet most cities boasted even fewer residents—on average, between five thousand and fifteen thousand people lived in Roman cities.

Cities were called *urbes* in Latin. Livy's monumental series pays homage to the importance of the city in Roman history. His collection is titled *Ab Urbe Condita*, which translates to *From the Founding of the City*.

Humble Beginnings

According to legend, Rome began with a collection of shepherds, escaped slaves, and men looking for a new start in life. Archaeologists have recently proven that during the eighth century BCE, the early Romans—whoever they were—definitely organized themselves and founded a city. Over the next few centuries, as history tells us, Rome expanded its rule to nearby cities and the rural areas they controlled.

Many of Rome's neighbors had a similar culture and spoke the same language, Latin, as the Romans. Other peoples of the area, such as the Etruscans, were quite different. Rome conquered them all, sometimes absorbing aspects of the conquered societies, but always imposing its own language, laws, and government.

As Rome's territory grew, so did the variety of cultures it incorporated. Southern Italy had many Greek settlements; northern Italy was the home of Celtic tribes (related to the Welsh and Irish of today). Outside of Italy, the Romans took over numerous well-established cities in eastern and southern regions such as Greece, Syria, and Egypt. There were far fewer urban areas in northwestern Europe. Where the Romans did not find cities, however, they created them. The Roman Empire embraced many languages and cultures, but all of the provinces under Roman rule came to have at least one thing in common: the importance of cities.

Rome, an Unrivaled City

"Goddess of continents and peoples, O Rome, whom nothing can equal and nothing approach"—this was how the Spanish-born poet Martial addressed the city he had adopted as his home. His feelings were shared by many. Rome was the largest and most powerful city in the Western world. It was not only the capital of the empire but was also a center of religion, literature, and culture. And it was home to more than a million people, a huge population for ancient times.

Rome reached its supreme status largely because of the great discipline, skill, and efficiency of the Roman army, for as the army won more territory, the city had more resources available to it. The Roman talent for organizing and engineering went hand in hand with this military might. When the soldiers of the Roman **legions** were not fighting, they were often at work on building projects, such as roads. These roads, in turn, made it easy for the legions, stationed throughout the empire, to receive supplies and deploy to trouble spots.

The impressive network of paved roads that connected the capital with the rest of the empire was not just for military use. Messengers to and from the emperor traveled with government communications. Students and tourists paid visits to the empire's great centers of learning and other famous sites. Merchants journeyed the roads with their carts and pack trains, loaded with olive oil, wine, cloth, produce, building materials, and other goods destined for the great city.

The Tiber River was another kind of roadway, linking Rome with the Mediterranean. From the port city of Ostia, barges made the 20-mile (32-kilometer) trip upriver to Rome bearing a world of luxurious imports: silk and spices from the East, marble and works of art from Greece and Asia Minor, pearls and rare purple dye from Syria, linen and glass from Egypt. The most important cargo of all, however, was grain, shipped from Sicily and North Africa. More than six million sacks of grain a year were required to feed the people of the city of Rome.

A sure food supply was one of Rome's greatest needs. Equally important was the water supply. Roman engineering guaranteed that fresh water was plentiful—in the amount of some 250 million gallons (950 million liters) a day. Eleven **aqueducts** brought this precious resource to the city from rivers and springs in the hills to the south and east. The water flowed in underground conduits or covered trenches for much of the way. To cross gorges and rivers, the conduits were laid over bridges supported by soaring arches. A water commissioner in 97 CE expressed the Romans' pride in these marvels of practical engineering in this way: "Will anybody compare the idle pyramids, or those other useless though renowned works of the Greeks with these aqueducts, these many indispensable structures?"

A Template for Success

Rome became the pattern for other cities in the empire. This was not so surprising in Italy, where generations of sharing a common culture naturally resulted in similar styles of building and urban development. Elsewhere, however, the Romans very deliberately promoted their own kind of urban lifestyle. For example, after southern Britain was conquered in the middle of the first century CE, Roman governors encouraged the native people to abandon their scattered rural settlements. The historian Tacitus described how his father-in-law, Agricola, governor of Britain for a number of years, used "the charms of luxury" to persuade his subjects to stop fighting the Romans and embrace city-based Roman ways:

> Agricola gave private encouragement and public aid to the building of temples, courts of justice, and dwelling-houses, praising the energetic, and reproving the indolent [lazy] … He likewise provided a liberal education for the sons of the chiefs … They who lately disdained the tongue of Rome now coveted its eloquence. Hence, too, a liking sprang up for our style of dress, and the "toga" became fashionable. Step by step they [the British people] were led to things which dispose to vice, the lounge, the bath, the elegant banquet. All this in their ignorance, they called civilization, when it was but a part of their servitude.

Where the Romans didn't have to build new cities, they often renovated and expanded existing ones. Emperors or wealthy citizens financed the construction of Roman-style temples, public buildings, marketplaces, bathhouses, monuments, and theaters in the cities of Greece, Asia Minor, and North Africa. Roman benefactors also frequently improved water supplies (by building aqueducts), harbor facilities, and the like. Such actions earned the gratitude of the cities' leading citizens, who were happy to enjoy these benefits of Roman rule.

By the second century CE, the Mediterranean world was dotted with "little Romes," cities whose architecture, language, money, and laws all expressed their belonging to the empire. A person from a city in Gaul (France) could visit a city in what is now western Turkey, more than 2,000 miles (3,200 km) away overland, and feel almost perfectly at home. Everyone paid for things with the same selection of silver, brass, and bronze coins; nearly everyone spoke either Latin or Greek. The surroundings were familiar: here would be the city center with its markets, law courts, and statues of the emperors; here were the temples dedicated to the deities that were worshipped all over the Roman world; here was an aqueduct supplying bathhouses and fountains.

The Romans called this cultural, political, and economic unity *pax Romana*, usually translated as "the Roman peace." But in the ancient world, "pax" meant not only a state of harmony but, more importantly, one of order, where everything worked according to "the rules"—that is, the Romans' rules.

ESTABLISHING ORDER

The Roman army played a major part in developing urban life throughout the empire. The army's first role in this process was, of course, conquering new territory for Rome. Then, if a new province already had well-established cities, the Roman government used them as headquarters to administer the province. If there were no urban settlements in desirable locations, the Romans built their own. Every legion included the surveyors, architects, carpenters, and stonemasons—along with the manpower provided by the ordinary soldiers—needed for any construction project.

One example of an army-built city is Timgad, in what is now northern Algeria. The emperor Trajan ordered its construction, in 100 CE, as a settlement for army veterans. These retired soldiers remained on reserve duty, and their town had a strategic location: its nearness to mountain passes allowed it to protect Roman-ruled territory from nomadic groups who lived to the south. The army planned and constructed Timgad carefully, with streets laid out in an orderly grid pattern. The city boasted all the comforts of Rome, including fourteen bathhouses.

Even without planning, the Roman legions were responsible for founding numerous cities, many of which still exist today. When the army set up an encampment or built a fort, people from all over the region were attracted to the area. The soldiers, who needed supplies, made excellent customers for local goods and produce. Taverns and other businesses were established to serve the army bases. Many legionnaires formed relationships with local women and had children with them; after the men were discharged from the army, they frequently settled with their families near the camp or fort. As the population grew, a city developed, and as such cities spread through a province, Roman culture—and control—were assured.

A GREAT CITY

It's difficult to imagine the evolution of Rome from a humble city into one of the greatest empires in world history. Livy himself seemed to marvel at the city's success, writing that he thought Rome to be second only to heaven.

In the next chapter, we'll look at what life was like for those living in a city full of marvels.

City Libraries

The idea of the public library was not a Roman innovation. Public libraries, including the Library of Alexandria, were first founded by the ancient Greeks. However, Roman emperors were eager to continue the tradition. Augustus alone established three public libraries in the city of Rome. Augustus's library located in the Atrium Libertatis is thought to be the first of the empire. Augustus was not the first emperor to make plans for a public library, though. Julius Caesar was in the process of planning a public library (he was even amassing books) at the time of his assassination.

These libraries were more than repositories for books. Historian T. Keith Dix has written extensively about public libraries in ancient Rome. According to Dr. Dix:

> We might … picture a crowd of listeners in Rome's libraries, for they seemed to have served as a setting for authors' recitations of their works, a fundamental form of "publication" in the ancient world. Providing a hall for a reading was one of the traditional responsibilities of an author's patron; making the public libraries available for recitations is one way for the founders to extend their literary patronage, just as the Ptolemies seem to have done in their library at Alexandria.

Therefore, public libraries were spaces for sharing ideas, both through physical books and public readings. Public libraries could be found in palaces, temples, forums, and even in public baths.

Chapter Two

The Urban Lifestyle

The Forum featured shops, courts of law, and temples.

"Having laid out the alleys and determined the streets, we
have next to treat of the choice of building sites for temples,
the forum, and all other public places, with a view to general
convenience and utility. If the city is on the sea, we should
choose ground close to the harbor as the place where the forum
is to be built; but if inland, in the middle of the town."
—Vitruvius

Cities in ancient Rome were carefully planned and featured paved
roads, fortifications, and numerous amenities. Architecture was
considered part art form, part science. One of the most famous
Roman architects is Marcus Vitruvius Pollio. Vitruvius, as he is
known, was an architect, engineer, and author. His ten-book series is referred
to as both *De Architectura* (its Latin name) and *The Ten Books on Architecture*.
In the series, Vitruvius set out to write a complete description of his chosen
field. He covers such topics as the education of an architect, the properties
of different kinds of timber and stone for building, the best place to establish
a city and its public buildings, and the proper proportions and designs for
temples to various gods and goddesses. Much of what we know about city
planning comes from the writings of Vitruvius.

CITY CENTER

From early times, the heart of Rome had been its Forum. In the middle of the Forum was a large rectangular plaza where citizens could gather for political meetings, business discussions, celebrations, ceremonies, and socializing. Around this open area were important temples, the Senate House and other government buildings, and the **basilica**, a spacious meeting hall where courts of law were held. There were also buildings that housed shops, offices, and schoolrooms. From a platform called the Rostra, emperors and senators made speeches to the people; when a notable person died, a relative might deliver a funeral **eulogy** from the Rostra. Inscriptions and painted notices on the walls of Forum buildings informed citizens of new laws, court decisions, and other important news. The Forum was also the ideal place to erect statues and monuments to honor the emperors and other famous Romans of both past and present.

As Rome grew, the original Forum became too small and crowded to serve the city's population. By 117 CE, five additional forums had been constructed nearby. The last, largest, and most splendid forum of all was built by the emperor Trajan, who paid for the whole thing from the riches of a recent conquest. The buildings in Trajan's forum included two libraries (one for books in Latin, the other for books in Greek) and a grand basilica paved with marble floors and roofed with tiles of gilded bronze. Beside the forum, Trajan had a marketplace constructed. An ancient version of a shopping mall, it housed around 150 shops, supplying the citizens of Rome with both luxuries and everyday needs.

Other cities in the empire had forums of their own. When the Romans took over a city or built a new city in conquered territory, constructing a forum was usually a priority. Forums were often expanded or renovated by emperors, sometimes as a gift when they were visiting a city. Prominent citizens also donated buildings and monuments to their city's forum. For example, one of the largest buildings in Pompeii's forum was a headquarters for the local wool-processing industry, given to the city and the woolworkers by a wealthy widow named Eumachia.

Out and About

Naturally, the forum was not the only place where a city's residents gathered. Just northeast of Rome's forums was the Campus Martius. This was described during the reign of Augustus by the Greek geographer Strabo as "an admirably large field on which an enormous number of chariots and horses can race unimpeded and a host of people can daily play ball games and practise discus-throwing and wrestling." The Campus was also the site of temples, tombs, and other monumental structures, as well as of occasional military drills. Many other Roman cities had similar athletic fields.

Nearly every urban neighborhood had a public well or fountain, near which people often lingered for a chat. Marketplaces were good locations for socializing as well as shopping. As in a modern city, friends or business associates frequently met up on the sidewalk; in some Roman cities, the sidewalks were shaded by roofs supported by columns. There were taverns, food stands, and cookshops, too.

Public bathhouses were among the favorite places for people to meet, whether to socialize or talk business. At one point there were more than eight hundred bathhouses in Rome alone. Many of them were huge, splendid buildings, decorated with colored marble and works of art. Public lavatories (which charged an entrance fee) were also favorite gathering places, for the Romans were experts at making a virtue of a necessity. A public restroom in an ancient Roman city usually had about twenty seats arranged in a semicircle or open rectangle. The seats were often of marble, and behind them, niches held statues of heroes, gods, and goddesses. Channels of constantly running water flowed under the seats to carry away sewage. In the middle of the bathroom there might be a fountain, and sometimes the room was heated by a furnace under the floor. For urban Romans, it seemed perfectly natural to sit down to a friendly conversation in these surroundings.

A Roman Bath

Bathing was an important part of a Roman's daily routine. Women usually bathed in the morning, while men bathed in the afternoon, before dinner. The very wealthy had bathing facilities in their homes, but most city dwellers went to a public bathhouse. The baths were open to everyone who could pay the small entrance fee, and sometimes admission was free, paid for by the emperor or some other dignitary.

A full Roman bath was an elaborate affair. Bathers undressed in a changing room that contained compartments for storing clothes. Then they went into a *sudatorium*, which was like a sauna or steam bath. After working up a sweat, they entered a room called the *caldarium*. Here they sprinkled themselves with hot water from a large tub and used a metal scraper to remove dirt and perspiration. (These hot rooms were heated by an underfloor furnace system called a *hypocaust*.) Next came the *tepidarium*, a warm room where bathers could begin to cool off. Then it was time to move on to the *frigidarium* for a plunge into a cold pool. The last stop was the *unctorium*, where they could be massaged and rubbed with oil.

Large bathhouses had facilities for exercising and socializing as well as for washing. Many had gymnasiums, exercise grounds, ball courts, and swimming pools. There might also be sculpture galleries, gardens, libraries, reading rooms, and rooms for gaming and conversation. Vendors and snack bars sold food and drink to bathers. For the Romans, a bath was as much a form of recreation as a way to get clean.

ROMAN APARTMENTS

The majority of Roman city dwellers probably spent as little time as possible in their homes, which tended to be small, dark, cold in the winter, and hot in the summer. There was rarely indoor plumbing—the great water supply brought in by the aqueducts was mainly for public use in fountains,

Housing and shops in the city of Pompeii

bathhouses, and lavatories. Artificial light was typically supplied by pottery lamps that burned olive oil, although candles might be used in provinces that didn't grow olives. The fireplace had not been invented yet; the usual heat source was a brazier, a kind of pan full of smoldering charcoal, supported by a tripod or other stand. Cooking was generally limited to whatever could be warmed by the brazier.

Such were the conditions in Roman apartment houses, which were called **insulae**, literally "islands." Like islands, these buildings rose up out of the urban "sea," three to five stories tall. A typical insula might house between thirty and fifty people. Some buildings had spacious apartments, with windows of mica, clear gypsum, or glass. There might be a central courtyard with a cistern, or tank, to hold water for the tenants' use. The remains of buildings like these are still standing in Ostia, and they are solidly constructed of concrete faced with brick. But a great many insulae were slums, shabbily constructed, with cramped apartments and nothing to cover the window openings except wooden shutters or oiled paper. The poet Juvenal wrote of such apartment buildings in Rome: "We inhabit a city propped up for the most part by slats: for that is how the landlord patches up the crack in the old wall, bidding the inmates sleep at ease under the ruin that hangs above their heads."

In more "upscale" insulae, the ground floor was often like a private house, occupied by the building's owner or rented by a single family. More commonly, the ground floor of an insula was devoted to stores or workshops, which were sometimes little more than booths opening to the street. In either case, this was the only floor that might have a lavatory; people in the upper stories had to make do with chamber pots, which they were supposed to empty into a vat under the stairs. Sometimes, however, people just dumped the contents of their chamber pots out the window; if they hit a passerby, however, they could be hauled into court and fined.

SINGLE-FAMILY HOMES

There were more than 46,000 insulae in the city of Rome, but only about 1,800 single-family houses—homes of the wealthy and privileged. Even in some of these, rooms on either side of the entryway were used as shops, often run or rented by slaves or freedmen of the family. (The shops were usually walled off from the rest of the building.) Otherwise the only opening on the front of the house was the door—for security and privacy, there were no windows looking out on the street.

The town houses of the wealthy, at least in Italy, generally followed a similar design. The entrance hall led into a large room called an **atrium**, which was used as a living room and a place to receive guests. Part of the atrium was unroofed, and beneath this opening was a rectangular pool to catch rainwater. Bedrooms and sitting rooms opened off the atrium. Toward the back, on either side, were recesses that housed small statues or paintings of the family's ancestors and protector gods. Behind the atrium was the tablinum, where the head of the family had his office. Next to the tablinum was a common location for the dining room. At the back of the house there was usually a peristyle, a courtyard or garden area surrounded by a covered walkway. Rooms opening off the peristyle might include the kitchen, slave quarters, storerooms, and sometimes a bath, a lavatory, and a stable. Really large and luxurious houses had even more rooms. For example, one lavish house in Pompeii had two atriums and two peristyles. There could also be an additional dining room, an extra room for entertaining, a picture gallery, a library, and elaborate gardens.

A family's wealth and culture were expressed by the way the house was decorated, with mosaic floors, frescoed walls, and elegant fountains and sculptures in the peristyle or garden. Mosaics were often done in abstract designs or geometric patterns, but sometimes they made elaborate pictures or spelled out messages (such as *Cave canem*, "Beware of the dog," found in many entryways). **Frescoes** could also be abstract, but often they showed landscapes or scenes from mythology. Dining rooms frequently had frescoes or mosaics depicting fruit, shellfish, or other types of food. This was an example of the Roman devotion to propriety, one of the most important elements of architecture according to Vitruvius, who called propriety "that perfection of style which comes when a work is authoritatively constructed on approved principles."

THE INFLUENCE OF ROMAN CITIES

Much about life in Roman cities sounds familiar: living in apartments, shopping and gathering in a central location, and even the building processes employed by Roman architects. On the other hand, customs like attending a public bath sound far removed to our modern ears. Yet both the familiar and strange aspects of life in Roman cities illuminate the reasons ancient Rome has had a lasting effect on our ideas of everyday life in cities.

Roman Building Innovations

In many cultures, the remnants of ancient structures have disappeared without a trace. Luckily for classicists, the same cannot be said of ancient Rome. Nearly everyone is familiar with the Colosseum and the Pantheon, which still exist in modern-day Rome. There are also aqueducts and temples in various states of preservation in the farther-flung reaches of the former empire: places like Lebanon and Croatia are home to vestiges of ancient Rome. The secret to the staying power of these sites lies in the Romans' building techniques.

Ancient Rome was one of the first civilizations to use concrete, and this development has allowed Roman buildings to stand the test of time. Roman concrete was not quite like the concrete of today. Professor David Moore explains it this way:

> The ancients hand mixed their components (wet lime and volcanic ash) in a mortar box with very little water to give a nearly dry composition, carried it to the job site in baskets placing it over a previously prepared layer of rock pieces, and then proceeded to pound the mortar into the rock layer. Fortunately, we have proof. Vitruvius, the noted Roman architect, mentioned this process in his [formulas] for his concrete, plus the fact that special tamping tools were used to build a cistern wall.

Today, engineers have begun studying the chemical composition of Roman concrete in the hopes of improving modern-day concrete, and historical sites provide invaluable information about Roman cities to archaeologists.

Chapter Three

Hard at Work

At times, slaves fought in gladiatorial matches, where the stakes were high: life or death.

"There is, to speak generally, no such thing as work without gain or gain without work: toil and pleasure, though apparent opposites, are indissolubly linked."

—Livy

Urban Romans held a vast array of jobs. Some worked as teachers, traders, and politicians. Others were merchants or craftsmen. Roman cities were home to entertainers, too. Athletes, actors, and musicians made their living in cosmopolitan Rome.

Romans woke up at sunrise because the lack of reliable artificial light sources meant fewer productive hours. After a quick breakfast of bread, water, and sometimes cheese, it was off to work. Many shopkeepers and craftsmen lived above their stores or in rooms behind them. However, most people had to walk through crowded city streets to get to their jobs.

On average, Romans finished up after about six hours (around lunch) and headed to the public baths. The Roman calendar featured many public holidays, which were observed with a respite from work. Of course, the majority of the Roman workforce was composed of slaves, and their lives did not include time off.

THE ROLE OF SLAVES

Slavery was a fact of life in the Roman Empire, as it was throughout the ancient world. It was very common to take huge numbers of captives from a country defeated in war, and for some time, Rome's conquests supplied the empire with most of its slaves. After the empire's borders became more settled, the majority of slaves were people born into slavery, for the children of slaves were also slaves.

Slaves were the backbone of Roman civilization.

Historians estimate that slaves made up about 30 percent of Rome's population. The city itself owned a number of slaves, who did administrative work, maintained the aqueducts, cleaned and repaired streets and public buildings, and worked on construction projects. Some wealthy Romans owned hundreds of slaves, and even people with modest incomes might have one or two. Some slaves worked in or even ran businesses for their masters; others were rented out to people who only needed a slave for a short time. Still other slaves were entertainers of one kind or another: gladiators, chariot racers, actors, singers, dancers, and acrobats. A large number of urban slaves worked in their owners' households as secretaries, accountants, librarians, doctors, midwives, wet nurses, teachers, hairdressers, barbers, maids, masseurs, cooks, launderers, housecleaners, doorkeepers, litter carriers, torchbearers, and so on.

The Roman economy was greatly dependent on slave labor. Keeping slaves from rebelling, therefore, was always a concern. Until the second half of the first century CE, slaves had no legal standing or protection, and owners could treat them however they wanted. Some masters used violence or the fear of violence to keep slaves obedient. We read of a cook being beaten for burning a meal and of a lady's maid having her hair pulled and her clothing torn for not curling her mistress's hair properly.

In 61 CE, a mistreated slave killed his master, a high-ranking city official in Rome. The victim's friends wanted all four hundred of his slaves put to death, to discourage other slaves who might think of murdering their owners. Many Romans protested against this cruel punishment. The Senate debated the matter and finally decided to allow the mass execution. As one senator put it, "You cannot control these dregs of society except through fear."

Other Romans, however, felt that it was better to treat slaves with some kindness and respect. Well-treated slaves who had the hope of eventually gaining their freedom were more likely to accept their state of servitude. Besides, some Romans argued, to treat slaves decently was simply the right and humane thing to do. This idea was expressed by the playwright-philosopher-statesman Seneca the Younger when he wrote to a friend:

> I was happy to learn from people who had just visited you that you live on friendly terms with your slaves … Some people say, "They're just slaves." But they are our fellow human beings! "They're just slaves."

But they live with us! "They're just slaves." In fact, they are our fellow slaves, if you stop to consider that fate has as much control over us as it has over them … I don't want to engage in a lengthy discussion of the treatment of slaves, toward whom we are very arrogant, very cruel, and very abusive. However, this is the essence of my advice: "Treat those of lower social rank as you would wish to be treated by those of higher social rank."

Household slaves were generally more fortunate than other slaves. Many were given an education or training in skilled crafts. Slaves who worked closely with their owners often had the opportunity to get to know them well, and a kind of friendship could grow between master and slave. Such slaves might receive gifts of money from their masters and even from their masters' friends; slaves were frequently able to save up enough to buy their freedom. Owners sometimes freed slaves out of gratitude for their service; it was very common for people to write a will that freed many or all of their slaves. There were even cases of childless couples freeing then adopting a favorite slave.

Freedmen and freedwomen often continued doing the same jobs they had performed as slaves. They still had to show loyalty and work a certain number of days a year for their former owners. But freed slaves became Roman citizens, with voting rights for the men. The children of freedmen were completely free and, if they were wealthy enough, could even run for public office and rise to the top ranks of Roman society. However, few attained this level of success.

The Sad Fact of Prejudice

Many of Rome's workers were freedmen or immigrants from Greek-speaking cities in the East. Some Romans resented these people contributing "foreign ideas" to society and "taking jobs away" from free citizens. The satirists Martial and Juvenal both expressed this prejudice, sometimes in an exaggerated manner. "Grammarian, **orator**, geometer, painter, wrestling-master, prophet, tightrope walker, medical man, wizard—he can do anything, your penniless Greek," Juvenal commented sarcastically. Martial complained:

> Fortune, do you really think this situation is fair? Maevius, who was not born in Syria or Parthia or bought at a Cappadocian slave auction, but who was native-born, … a citizen who is pleasant, honest, a blameless friend, who knows both Latin and Greek … shivers in a cheap gray garment, while Incitatus, a freedman, a former mule driver, shines forth in scarlet.

AN INDUSTRIOUS POPULATION

In a Roman city, a large number of jobs could be done by slaves, freedmen, or freeborn people of the lower class. Regardless of their status as free or slave, workers in the same craft or trade banded together in some cities to form what we might call guilds. These associations hosted dinners for their members and often paid members' funeral expenses. Like modern trade unions, the guilds also endorsed political candidates. Graffiti from walls in the southern Italian city of Pompeii campaigned to passersby with slogans such as, "The muleteers urge the election of Gaius Julius Polybius."

The goods produced in Roman cities might be used locally or shipped to other parts of the empire. Many Romans were skilled artisans, among them leatherworkers, woodworkers, stoneworkers, and metalworkers. Some produced luxury items such as dyes, cosmetics, perfumes, jewelry, mosaics, furniture, wall paintings, and garden ornaments. Numerous shops were small individual or

Some artisans' work has stood the test of time, like this mosaic of gladiators.

family businesses, where the artisan both made and sold goods in the same place. There were also large workshops or factories employing many people, which produced a variety of foodstuffs and manufactured goods, for example fish sauce, olive oil, wine, pottery, lamps, bricks, glassware, and cloth. Providing food and drink kept numerous city workers busy, including bakers, butchers, fishmongers, chicken sellers, innkeepers, and snack-bar operators. Then there were auctioneers, town criers, carters, porters, water carriers, boatmen, bathhouse attendants, sewer cleaners, construction workers, veterinarians—the list of occupations could go on and on. In addition, in many urban areas some people went out every day to work on farms outside the city limits.

Even with so many jobs to do, however, there were people who couldn't get work, especially in Rome. Some worked as day laborers or did odd jobs. Even some workers with full-time employment could not earn enough to support their families. Urban rents were very high, and so were other prices. For example, a pound of chicken could cost a tailor a full day's wages; a pair of boots for a mule driver cost him nearly five days' earnings. Freeborn workers had no healthcare plans, unemployment insurance, or other job benefits. For all of these reasons, free Romans sometimes had a much harder time than many slaves whose masters provided them with food, clothing, housing, and medical care.

A Diverse Workforce

From slaves to lawyers, everyone in a Roman city had a job to do. While some women certainly worked outside of their homes (and there was a sizable population of female slaves), most industries were a man's world. In the next chapter, we'll explore the day-to-day lives of these urban men.

Fast Food

Much like today, making and selling food was a big business in ancient Rome. City dwellers in the ancient empire rarely had access to a kitchen in their homes, which made restaurants a critical industry. Called both *tabernae* and *cauponae*, these restaurants often specialized in serving food to go. Today, scholars often classify them as "snack bars." Many even had counters that resemble modern fast food establishments. They were conveniently located for their patrons—it wasn't unusual to see a taberna inside of an apartment building.

Bakeries were also plentiful. Shops offered loaves of bread and desserts and were unique to Roman cities. (In the countryside, most Romans baked at home instead of buying what they needed.) Feeding urban Romans was a tall order. Archaeologists believe that at the height of the empire, there were around 250 bakeries in the city of Rome alone. Baking was the kind of hands-on profession that was passed down from father to son.

CHAPTER FOUR
CITY MEN

This third-century-CE sarcophagus demonstrates the pivotal role Roman fathers played in their children's lives.

"All nations and cities are ruled by the people,
the nobility, or by one man."

—Tacitus

I n Rome, the people were ruled by one man: the emperor. Yet this rule
was overshadowed on the family level by the man of the house. The
paterfamilias, "father of a family," was the head of the household, with
absolute authority over every member of his family. A father had legal
control over his daughters and sons until his death. Therefore, if an adult male's
father was still alive, that male would be financially dependent on his father.
The paterfamilias provided his sons with an allowance, called a *peculium*, which
was used to fund his sons' lifestyles. At times, fathers and sons argued over
this money. Regardless, fathers were eager to pass on their name and therefore
prized sons above daughters. Ideas about a man's role in Roman society shaped
both family life and the governance of the empire. The state was thought of as
a very large extended family, which the emperor was supposed to oversee like
a stern but caring father. Even the ruling class, the patricians, got their name
from ideals about fatherhood: *patricii* means "those with fatherly qualities."

The Patronage System

Another word related to *pater* ("father") was *patronus*, "defender." In ancient Rome, a patronus, or patron, was a man whom a number of other men depended on to look out for their interests, advise them, help them in times of trouble, give them gifts, and so on. These were the patron's clients. They, in turn, owed the patron loyalty and various services, such as accompanying him to the forum when he had important business there or campaigning and voting for him in local elections. The more clients a man had, the more influence he had, and the higher his status was. One of the reasons that the emperor Augustus was able to rise to power was that he had a huge number of clients, probably more than any other man in Rome.

Freed slaves became their former masters' clients. Freeborn men also had patrons, and even a patron with a number of clients would have a patron of his own, a man of higher rank. Patronage was a kind of ladder, where every man was a client of someone on the rung above him. At the top of the ladder was the emperor. He alone had no patron, except perhaps Jupiter, the chief god of the Roman state.

Almost the first thing a Roman man did after getting up was go to wish his patron good morning. This visit was a show of respect, and the patron might have some errand or task he wanted a client to do. The client generally hoped to receive a gift or handout, or perhaps a dinner invitation. Most patrons invited their clients to dinner now and then, and often this was the only time a poor man had a really good meal. A stingy or arrogant patron, however, might serve his clients inferior food and drink, while higher-ranking guests at the same dinner joined the host in a meal of the best quality.

Pliny the Younger on the Peculium

Roman author Pliny the Younger had strong beliefs about fatherhood. In a letter to his friend Junior, he expressed his conviction that fathers should be guided by empathy:

> A certain individual rebuked his son for buying horses and dogs which cost a little too much. When the young fellow had gone off, I said to his father: "Come on now, did you never do anything deserving a rebuke from your father? I put that in the past tense, but do you not sometimes act in a way which your son would censure as harshly if he suddenly turned father, and you turned son? Aren't we all misguidedly drawn into one mistake or another? Don't different people indulge themselves in different ways?"

> Many scholars have cited this passage in their discussion of the peculium. Historians see Pliny's views as proof that many fathers were generous and understanding when it came to their son's allowance. Others argue that the peculium did not play a long-term role in a man's life—life expectancy was short enough in ancient Rome that many men's fathers died before the men were too far into adulthood themselves.

THE WEALTHIEST ROMANS

Men with the rank of senator were at the top of Roman society. They did not have to work for a living; in fact, it was actually illegal for them to earn money through their own labor. Senators were the great landowners of the empire, and most of their income came from the sale of the produce on their farming

The Roman Senate

estates. With agents acting for them, members of the senatorial class also profited from property rentals, business investments, and moneylending.

Because senators were the wealthiest of Roman citizens, they were expected to devote themselves to government service. And only the rich could afford to serve in the government: not only were officeholders unpaid, but they were expected to spend a great deal of their own money on public works, entertainments, and gifts to the common people. Even when they served as lawyers, they worked for free.

One of the most important senators in Rome was the city prefect, who was appointed by the emperor. Responsible for maintaining law and order, he commanded the urban cohort, as many as 4,500 soldiers who formed a kind of police force. The city prefect also inspected markets to make sure meat prices were fair, and he had the power to prohibit individuals from engaging in business, professional, or legal activities.

Below the senators ranked the **equestrians**. To belong to this class, a man did not have to be as wealthy as a senator, but he was still far richer than the majority of people in the empire. Equestrians were typically involved in "big business," making money as importers and exporters, ship owners, bankers, bidders on government contracts, and the like. Some military and government positions were open to equestrians, and these opportunities increased as the empire went on.

While Rome's government was in the hands of the emperor and his appointees, in many other cities of the empire, men of the upper classes could run for election to town offices. The graffiti from Pompeii show that local political life could be quite lively. Elections were held every year to choose two *duovirs*, or co-mayors, and an *aedile*, who supervised the markets, public buildings, and public works. Often there was also some kind of town council, made up of wealthy freeborn men.

The Life of a Soldier

Soldiers were a familiar sight in Roman cities—but not always a welcome sight. In camp, soldiers lived according to strict discipline, but when they were out on the town they had a reputation for bullying civilians. Since a soldier could only be disciplined by his commander, a civilian filing a complaint had little hope of justice, as Juvenal pointed out in one of his *Satires*:

> Your teeth are shattered? Face hectically inflamed, with great black welts? You know the doctor wasn't too optimistic about the eye that was left. But it's not a bit of good your running to the courts about it. If you've been beaten up by a soldier, better keep it to yourself.

For some 125,000 to 165,000 men, the army was their career for most of their lives. The requirements for joining the Roman legions were strict. Recruits had to be Roman citizens, and they had to meet high standards of physical fitness. They had to be mentally tough, too, with a strong team spirit, and for good reason: When the army was on campaign, the soldiers lived in leather tents, eight men to a tent. On the march, each group of eight shared a mule, which carried the tent and some supplies. The men themselves carried not only their weapons but also the necessary equipment for any construction projects they might have to undertake. The first-century-CE historian Josephus described a Roman legion on the march this way:

> Then they march forward, everyone silent and in correct order, each man maintaining his particular position in the ranks, just as he would in battle. The infantry are equipped with breastplates and helmets, and carry a sword on both sides … The infantry chosen to guard the general carry a spear and a small round shield. The rest of the soldiers carry a javelin and an oblong shield. However, they also carry a saw, a basket, a shovel, and an ax, as well as a leather strap, a scythe, a chain, and three days' food rations. As a result, an infantryman differs little from a loaded pack mule.

Serving in the Roman legions was far more of a commitment than enlisting in a modern army. Once a man joined up, he was required to stay for twenty-five years. If he deserted and was caught, he was executed. Discipline was harsh, and training was rigorous. The cost of a soldier's armor, equipment, and food was deducted from his pay. Legions were generally stationed near the empire's frontiers, or in trouble spots far from Italy. Moreover, until 197 CE, legionary soldiers were not allowed to marry (although they frequently had long-term, but unofficial, relationships with women who lived near the army bases).

The army offered some opportunities for promotion. An ambitious man might rise to the rank of centurion, a commander who earned as much as sixty times the pay of ordinary legionnaires. Retired centurions often became important, respected men in their communities. Every soldier who survived his twenty-five years of service received a retirement bonus that equaled close to fourteen years' pay. The hope of such rewards was enough to make the army an appealing career choice for many men, especially those who had few other opportunities. The historian Tacitus, a senator during the first century CE, remarked on this fact a little scornfully: "It is chiefly the needy and the homeless who adopt by their own choice a soldier's life."

A centurion

Masculine Ideals

Men in ancient Rome led lives charged with potential. Even slaves had the opportunity to rise to higher social ranks. Men were the heart of their families, and in their own homes, their word was law. Historians have been able to reconstruct a clear view of the rights and responsibilities of Roman men thanks to primary sources. We know that fatherhood was critically important in the empire. Alternatively, the lives of Roman women weren't as well documented as those of their male counterparts. The following chapter presents what we *do* know about women in the Roman Empire.

CHAPTER FIVE
CITY WOMEN

Wealthy Roman women were attended
by slaves.

"Agrippina herself was determined, and rather excitable.
But she turned this to good account by
her devoted faithfulness to her husband."

—Tacitus

Upper-class Roman women were expected to be dutiful wives
and mothers. While some worked (a few notable women even
owned their own businesses), most had a limited education
and married in their early teens. City women were tasked with
running a respectable household, whether their families lived in an insula or
a **domus**. Responsibilities included shopping for the whole family and raising
children. Many women also made textiles.

A woman's lifestyle depended greatly on her social class. Upper-class
women often had power, though it was always expressed behind the scenes.
Alternatively, female slaves lived difficult lives.

WOMEN WITH STATUS

The amount—and kind—of freedom a woman enjoyed depended largely on
her wealth and social class. An upper-class woman had many slaves to help
her in the home, so she was able to go out to visit friends, exercise and relax

at the baths, or attend public shows. She could also spend her leisure time reading, playing board games, or playing a musical instrument. A few upper-class women wrote poetry or other works, though little of these survive. Many Roman men, however, were offended if women showed too much intelligence, as Juvenal expressed in his *Satires*: "Don't marry a woman who speaks like an orator—or knows every history book. There should be some things in books which she doesn't understand. I hate a woman who … always obeys all the laws and rules of correct speech, who quotes verses I've never even heard of."

The ideal for Roman women, especially of the upper classes, was often portrayed in funeral eulogies such as this one for a woman named Murdia: "My dearest mother won the greatest praise of all, because she was like other good women in her modesty, decency, chastity, obedience, wool-work, zeal and loyalty." These were the qualities that Roman men valued most in wives, mothers, and daughters. Wool-working, by the way, was traditionally women's main work: spinning thread, weaving cloth, and sewing the family's clothes. In the early empire, many upper-class women still did these things themselves; later, they usually only oversaw the wool-working of their household slaves.

An upper-class Roman woman's main duty was to bear and raise children. This was, in fact, a dangerous job. Even with the best doctor or midwife, there was a lot that could go wrong during pregnancy and childbirth, and a large number of mothers and babies died. Miscarriages were also common. Many women had trouble getting pregnant in the first place. For all of these reasons, most upper-class women had only one to three children, even though large families were the ideal.

PLEBEIAN WOMEN

While women of the upper classes enjoyed freedom from hard work, they had little control over their personal lives. Their marriages were always arranged, frequently for the sake of financial or political advantages for their fathers. For the same reasons, fathers could (and did) order daughters to divorce and then marry men with better connections. Divorce was not unusual in ancient Rome, and the children remained with their father.

In contrast, lower-class women might choose their own husbands. We have many examples of tombstones belonging to couples who met while they were slaves. Slaves were not allowed to marry, but people formed lasting relationships anyway. A slave who was freed often bought the freedom of his or her partner so that the two could be legally married. Freed slaves and freeborn workers alike might meet future spouses among their coworkers in shops or factories. Among poorer Romans, there was more opportunity for marriage to be based on love and friendship, since political and financial influences were not an issue.

Poorer Romans, however, had to work hard to earn a living. Many women worked only in the home, spinning, weaving, sewing, cooking, cleaning, and raising their children. Sometimes they sold some of the thread they spun or pieces of cloth they wove. Other women might assist their husbands in home-based family businesses. Still others held jobs outside the home or had their own businesses. This may have been especially true of freedwomen, who had often learned and practiced various trades while slaves.

The evidence for Roman working women often makes it difficult to tell if they were slaves, freedwomen, or freeborn women; probably women of all three groups frequently worked side by side, and oftentimes labored alongside men, too. Historians have learned that women worked at a variety of crafts and trades; among others, we know of women who were weavers, menders, dye makers, doctors, midwives, wet nurses, maids, secretaries, hairdressers, dressmakers, perfumers, actresses, dancers, innkeepers, waitresses, bathhouse attendants, shopkeepers, fruit and vegetable sellers, fishmongers, moneylenders, and property owners.

Divorce in the Ancient World

Divorce was a standard occurrence in ancient Rome. A Roman man could divorce his wife for a number of reasons, and the process itself was easy. Divorce was so commonplace that, according to historians Lesley Adkins and Roy Adkins:

> About one in six upper-class marriages ended in divorce in the first ten years, another one in six ended through the death of one spouse … Remarriage was fairly frequent. Many men remarried without difficulty after divorce, although it was more difficult for a divorced woman to remarry.
>
> To divorce, a couple would state their intention in front of seven witnesses. This witnessed statement concluded their marriage. Women were entitled to their dowry in most circumstances. Toward the end of the empire, women also gained the right to initiate a divorce.

WOMEN WHO WROTE

For the most part, literary activities (besides reading) were for men. We do know of a small number of women, though, who were writers. One of these was Sulpicia, who lived in Rome toward the end of the first century BCE. Only fragments of a few of Sulpicia's poems survive.

Another literary woman was Pamphila of Epidaurus, Greece, who lived around the middle of the first century CE. The daughter of a learned man, she married a scholar and became extremely interested in history. Pamphila wrote thirty-three books of history, which were much read even a hundred years after her death. They are lost now, but a ninth-century author still knew of Pamphila and summarized her introduction to her work:

> She says that after thirteen years of living with her husband since she was a child, she began to put together these historical materials and recorded what she had learned from her husband during those thirteen years … and whatever she happened to hear from anyone else visiting him (for there were many visitors with a reputation for learning). And she added to this what she had read in books.

This reading woman has been immortalized in bronze.

We can assume—or at least hope—that there were other women like Pamphila who enjoyed the satisfactions of learning. Yet women's limited access to education is the very reason so little is known about their lives. Overall, male authors did not think that women were a worthy topic. In chapter 6, we'll examine the lives of another demographic that was often overlooked: children.

CHAPTER SIX

CHILDHOOD IN THE CITY

A young girl playing a popular game that is similar to the modern game of jacks

"One is not born wise, but becomes wise."

—Seneca the Younger

Childhood in ancient Rome was fairly short lived. Upper-class girls began to marry in their early teens, and boys were considered adults at the age of sixteen. A child's younger years differed wildly based on social class. Wealthy children (boys and girls) often attended school. On the other hand, children whose families were of lower classes began working at a young age. Yet childhood in a Roman city was not wholly different from childhood today: children played with toys and families took advantage of the rich experiences city life had to offer.

New Life

All Roman babies were born at home. After birth, the child was laid at its father's feet. If the father picked up the baby, it would be raised by the family. Otherwise, the child was exposed—taken outside and left in some public place to die or to be found and raised by someone else. Occasionally, an abandoned baby might be taken in by a childless couple who would truly love and care for it. More often, people who picked up these children were slave dealers.

This was one of the harsh facts of life among the Roman poor: parents who already had more children than they could afford to feed sometimes felt they had no choice but to expose their newborn. There were no reliable methods of family planning, no foster-care systems, and no adoption agencies. The lack of advanced medical treatments also led people to abandon babies with birth defects. And fathers rejected female infants more often than males, since boys would have a greater ability to contribute to the family income.

Historians cannot be certain how common it was for babies to be abandoned during the first two centuries of the empire. It was an ancient custom, and there were no laws against it. A letter has been found from Roman-ruled Egypt, written in 1 BCE by a husband who had to leave his family to find work. He wrote home to his pregnant wife, "If I receive my pay soon, I will send it up to you. If you have the baby before I return, if it is a boy, let it live; if it is a girl, expose it."

EDUCATION AND PLAY

Even a baby who wasn't exposed was not sure to survive. Roughly 25 percent of Roman infants died during their first year, and perhaps 25 percent of those who made it to age one died by age ten. So the survival of a healthy child, in a family with the means to care for it, was a source of great joy. Parents generally did all they could to ensure that their children thrived, even taking precautions against supernatural forces. For example, most Roman children wore a bulla, a circular pendant made of gold (for the well-off) or leather (for the poor), for protection against evil spirits.

Like children throughout history, Roman children liked toys, games, pets, and sweet treats. Boys and girls in wealthy families, of course, had more opportunities to enjoy these things. Some of the toys available were dolls (made of rags, wood, or bone), model chariots, tops, marbles, hobbyhorses, and wooden swords. There were board games resembling backgammon and checkers. Another game, knucklebones, usually played with the anklebones of goats, may have been like jacks. Then there were games similar to hide-and-seek, leapfrog, and blindman's buff. A wide variety of ball games could be enjoyed by children of all ages.

Children's education usually began at home. Parents taught manners, moral principles, and religious beliefs, and probably told stories about their ancestors and great heroes of the past. In prosperous families, trusted slaves also took part in raising and teaching the children. Many wealthy children, particularly boys, were educated at home by private tutors for years. Other boys, and some girls, began attending elementary school around the age of seven.

Wax tablets could be "erased" and reused, so they were often employed by students learning to write.

The school day began as soon as it was light out. Students went home for lunch at midday but might have more classes afterward. Schools were usually held in shops, small apartments, or public places such as the forum or even on the sidewalk. Students might have chairs, but there were no desks. Sometimes books were used, and the pupils had wooden tablets coated with wax; they used a writing instrument called a stylus to scratch their exercises into the wax. Oftentimes the teacher would simply recite literary passages to the students, who memorized and recited them back. Many teachers beat students who did poorly. Enlightened educators, such as the orator Quintilian, recommended a different approach for teaching a child:

> Let his lessons be fun, let him volunteer answers, let him be praised, and let him learn the pleasure of doing well. If, on occasion, he refuses instruction, bring in someone to serve as a rival, someone with whom he can compete; but let him think that he is doing well more often than not. Encourage him with the rewards or prizes in which his age group delights.

In elementary school, children learned basic reading, writing, and arithmetic. They also memorized legends, laws, poems, and wise sayings. This was where schooling ended for most Romans—there was no free public education, and most parents could not afford to pay a schoolteacher for more than a few years, if that. Some boys, however, went on to grammar school around the age of ten or eleven. Here they polished their writing ability, studied public speaking and poetry, and learned Greek (if they didn't already know it). They might also study some astronomy, science, music, and philosophy. At the age of fourteen or fifteen, a few boys—usually only those from the upper classes—received advanced training in public speaking and law.

Pets in Ancient Rome

It wasn't unusual for Roman families to keep pets, though the list of domesticated animals preferred in ancient times includes some unusual picks. Primary sources indicate that monkeys, snakes, and even weasels served as companions. Of course, more standard choices had a place in Roman families: dogs were the most common pet of the era. Evidence suggests that the Romans enjoyed the company of many breeds of dog. Not all of these breeds still exist today, but some do. Roman women were known to prefer the Maltese in particular.

Pets were sometimes memorialized with their owners in funerary sculptures.

Some pets had practical purposes, such as limiting the population of mice or other indoor pests. Others, like birds, were prized solely for their companionship. Many scholars say that Romans kept birds of all types and especially enjoyed breeds that could talk. Historians have discovered a Roman text warning bird owners to watch their language in front of their pet so that the bird did not pick up any bad habits!

In fact, Romans wrote extensively about their love of animals. Other than these texts, it's easy to see pets' prominent role in children's lives in the artwork of the time.

Growing Up Quickly

Adult responsibilities came early to most Romans. Slave children and children from very poor families might start working by the age when others were going to elementary school. For example, we have this gravestone inscription for a girl who made women's hairnets: "Viccentia, sweetest daughter, maker of gold nets, who lived for nine years and nine months." Even most boys who went to elementary school probably started working for a living before they were teenagers. If a father practiced a skilled craft or trade, he generally taught it to his sons, who then worked alongside him. Other boys might serve an apprenticeship learning a trade from a neighbor or relative. Many boys had no chance to learn any skills and had to take whatever work they could get.

A boy officially became an adult at around sixteen. The day he came of age was usually one of celebration. First the boy left his bulla and his purple-bordered childhood toga at the shrine of his family's protector deities. Then he put on the pure white toga of manhood. After a visit to the forum, his family and friends gave him a party. If he belonged to the upper classes, he was now able to begin his career in government or business. A lower-class boy could now join the army if he wanted to.

There was no coming-of-age ceremony for girls. After elementary school (if they got to attend at all), they began preparing for marriage, learning the skills they would need to run a household. By the time a girl was a teenager, she was usually married, or at least engaged, especially if she belonged to the upper classes. (Daughters of wealthy families tended to marry in their early teens, or even younger; women of the lower classes might not marry till their mid to late teens.) Her father or guardian chose her husband, who was generally quite a bit older than she was; he might even be in his forties or fifties and have been married before.

The night before her wedding, the bride gave away her toys to younger friends and relatives and laid her bulla in the family shrine. Very early on the wedding morning, her mother dressed her in her bridal garments, which included a yellow-orange veil crowned with a wreath of flowers. The wedding ceremony took place in the bride's home, with the couple joining hands and stating their consent to be married. In the evening, after a banquet, a lively torchlit procession escorted the bride to her new home. After she was carried over the threshold (for good luck), two bridesmaids brought in her distaff and spindle, with which she would spin wool, symbolizing her new life as a married woman.

A Short but Sweet Childhood

Life expectancy was part of the reason that children transitioned to adulthood so quickly in ancient Rome. By and large, Romans lived only into their thirties—life in the ancient world involved danger and disease. Of course, there were upsides to the Roman way of life. One such benefit was the free time between work, school, and chores. Chapter 7 takes a closer look at how urban Romans relaxed.

Chapter Seven

Leisure Pursuits

Roman men gathered at taverns to socialize with their friends.

> "Really I think that the characteristic and peculiar vices of this
> city, a liking for actors and a passion for gladiators and horses,
> are all but conceived in the mother's womb."
>
> —Tacitus

The Roman calendar featured well over one hundred holidays a year. These holidays marked religious occasions and provided a respite from work. Though Romans did not observe a weekend, holidays, festivals, and a relatively short workday meant that free Romans had quite a bit of free time. During their time off, men visited taverns or snack bars. There they would pass the time drinking, gambling, and talking. Respectable women did not go to taverns, but they could attend dinner parties and similar private social functions.

FEASTS AND PARTIES

Dinnertime arrived in late afternoon. Poor people usually ate very simply, sitting on stools in their apartments and perhaps having little more than porridge and beans, unless they were invited to dine at their patron's home. For

A banquet might include rare foods like peacock.

well-to-do Romans, giving or attending a dinner party was a favorite form of recreation. These dinners might be relatively small and simple, or they could be lavish banquets with exotic foods and elaborate entertainment. In good weather, they were often held outside in the garden or peristyle.

A Roman dining room or outdoor dining area typically contained three couches arranged around a low table. Diners reclined, leaning on their left elbows, three to a couch. They ate with spoons, knives, and their fingers. Slaves waited on them and brought them water for hand washing whenever necessary. For some special outdoor dinners, the couches were set around a garden pool, and the guests selected morsels of food from boat-shaped floating dishes.

A Roman dinner generally had three courses, but there could be several dishes in each course. First came appetizers, which were often egg dishes, fish, and raw vegetables. The main course featured meats and cooked vegetables. Choices for dessert included fruit, pastries, and cakes. The usual drink was wine.

The entertainment during and after a meal depended on the host's wealth and tastes. Many diners were satisfied simply with good conversation. Slaves often provided music while guests were eating. Between courses there might be performances by singers, dancers, actors, or acrobats. Upper-class men with literary interests often held recitations as part of the after-dinner entertainment. They would read aloud from their own writings, or from the works of famous authors.

Clients were expected to attend recitations by their patron (and to praise him enthusiastically), and many men felt that going to recitations was a boring duty. Others, however, looked forward to these literary dinners, as Pliny the Younger wrote in one of his letters: "I scarcely ever miss a recitation. Of course, usually the people reciting are friends of mine; for there is almost no one who is fond of literary studies who is not also fond of me."

ANCIENT ENTERTAINMENT

The Romans referred to several different kinds of events as *ludi*, or games, including plays and other theatrical presentations. Plays were modeled on Greek comedies and tragedies, and only men acted in them. **Pantomimes** were more popular but also less respectable because they included female performers and appealed to the senses with music, dance, beautiful costumes and scenery, and lively action. Pantomimes may have been a little like ballets, since the performers acted out stories—usually based on familiar myths and legends—without using words. Quintilian wrote about how skilled and expressive the performers could be: "Their hands demand and promise, they summon and dismiss; they translate horror, fear, joy, sorrow … They excite and they calm. They implore and they approve. They possess a power of imitation which replaces words."

Holidays and Festivals

Roman holidays were abundant and often celebrated with a visit to a temple. Here are some of the major festivals (you might recognize one or two!):

January 1: A day to commemorate the god Janus

February 13–21: A festival held to honor deceased ancestors

April 28–May 3: A spring festival

June 11: A festival to celebrate mothers

July 23: A festival honoring Neptune

September 23: The festival of Apollo

The January 1 festival resembled our modern-day celebration of the new year. The god Janus was depicted with two faces, one looking forward and the other looking back. (Janus represented the past and present.) Romans often marked the day with presents. Lamps were a popular gift because they were meant to help recipients navigate the new year.

The Matralia on June 11 was not quite parallel to today's Mother's Day. This festival was limited to women married to their first husband, and slaves were excluded from the celebration, too. Furthermore, women were expected to pray for their nieces and nephews instead of their own children.

Rome's oldest and most beloved form of popular entertainment was chariot racing. Races were held on a narrow oval track in an oblong roofless building called a **circus**. By the end of the second century CE, there were eight circuses in and around the city of Rome alone; the largest of these, the Circus Maximus, had room for 250,000 spectators. In cities throughout the empire, chariot racing was highly organized. There were four racing factions, or teams, named

The City in the Roman Empire

after the colors of their uniforms: Greens, Blues, Reds, and Whites. The same four colors were used wherever there was a circus, even though, for example, the Greens in Rome had a different owner and drivers than the Greens in Pompeii. The faction owners owned not only the chariots, horses, and stables, but also most of the drivers. Every faction had die-hard fans who sat together in the circus to cheer for their team and root against the other factions. Sometimes fans of different factions even got into fistfights during a race.

Chariot racing was an exciting sport. The course was long and narrow, with tight left-hand turns at each end. The lightweight chariots, made of wicker or wood, might be pulled by two to ten horses, although most races were for four-horse chariots. The drivers used whips to urge their horses through seven laps around the track. (In the Circus Maximus, this made for a race of about 2.5 miles, or 4 kilometers.) Crashes, injuries, and even deaths among both horses and drivers were common—but for the spectators, this element of danger only added to the excitement.

A retiarius wields his trident during a gladiatorial match

Even bloodier games took place in the empire's **amphitheaters**. These nearly circular open-air stadiums were the scenes of gladiator combats and wild-animal fights. Gladiators were usually slaves or prisoners of war. They were trained to fight in specific styles; for example, a retiarius was a gladiator who fought with a net and trident, while a Thracian used a curved sword and round shield. Most fights were not necessarily to the death, although a gladiator certainly could be killed or mortally injured during the course of combat.

On the other hand, amphitheater shows also included executions, in which condemned criminals were sent to fight gladiators or wild animals. Those who received this sentence went into the **arena** unarmed, and they did not come out alive.

One of the world's most famous buildings, the Colosseum in Rome, was an amphitheater. When the emperor Titus opened it in 80 CE, he sponsored one hundred days of elaborate spectacles, as reported by the senator and historian Dio Cassius:

> There was a battle between cranes and also between four elephants; animals both tame and wild were slain to the number of nine thousand; and women (not those of any prominence, however) took part in despatching them. As for the men, several fought in single combat and several groups contended together both in infantry and naval battles. For Titus suddenly filled this same theatre with water and brought in horses and bulls and some other domesticated animals that had been taught to behave in the liquid element just as on land. He also brought in people on ships, who engaged in a sea-fight there.

Not all Romans enjoyed these types of events. Seneca the Younger, for one, was highly critical of their influence. He wrote to a friend, "There is nothing more harmful to one's character than attendance at some spectacle, because vices more easily creep into your soul while you are being entertained. When I return home from some spectacle, I am greedier, more aggressive … I am more cruel and inhumane." Most people today would agree with Seneca—but for a great many ancient Romans, it seems that amphitheater events gave them a welcome escape from their own poverty and powerlessness.

"Fate may spare you many times; she gets you in the end."
—Seneca the Younger

Imagine the largest city in the world in the year 100 BCE, well before public transportation, building codes, or effective sanitary measures (like indoor plumbing). Though the city of Rome—and other cities around the empire—was considered cutting edge in its day, it was still plagued by problems. A Roman city could be a difficult and even dangerous place to live.

DANGER AHEAD

Crime, crowding, noise, pollution, poverty, unemployment—cities everywhere have suffered from such problems. In the ancient world, some of these troubles were especially bad. For example, with no streetlights of any kind, it was very easy for thieves to sneak up on pedestrians at night. Not surprisingly, Roman city dwellers rarely went out after dark; if they had to, slaves or hired boys carried torches to light the way. Nighttime travelers who were poor rarely had these options. And thieves were not the only hazard, since it was difficult for people to even see where they were going in the darkness.

Along with kitchen garbage and other trash, urban pollution included sewage and animal manure. These wastes accumulated in alleyway cesspits and dung heaps, posing a constant threat to public health—and a persistent assault to the nose. While Rome and many other cities did have wonderful sewer systems for the time, the sewers mainly drained bathhouses and public lavatories, and they emptied the wastewater and untreated sewage into the nearest river.

The water system—excellent as it was, coming from the countryside—also posed a danger; since lead pipes were frequently used, it is likely that a great number of Roman city dwellers suffered from lead poisoning. Lead was also an ingredient in some women's cosmetics—even makeup had its perils. Many Romans, however, did realize that lead was harmful; Vitruvius wrote, "Water ought by no means to be conducted in lead pipes, if we want to have it wholesome." Unfortunately, Vitruvius's advice was largely ignored.

Disease was inescapable for rich and poor alike, although the poor were especially susceptible to illnesses caused by malnutrition and poor sanitation. But even for the wealthy, there were no vaccines, antibiotics, or advanced surgical procedures. There were also no standards of education for doctors. Good ones learned their profession by apprenticing to skilled physicians. Anyone, however, could claim to be a doctor, without any training at all. The most experienced doctors were still unable to cure a great number of illnesses. The average life expectancy for ancient Romans was only twenty-seven years.

FIRE AND OTHER DISASTERS

Cities, with their crowded conditions, were highly vulnerable to epidemics and other disasters. One of the calamities most feared by city dwellers was fire. Spreading easily from building to building, a fire could wipe out whole neighborhoods in a very short time. Rome itself suffered several catastrophic fires. The worst one occurred in 64 CE, during the reign of the emperor Nero. Tacitus described it:

> The blaze in its fury ran first through the level portions of the city, then rising to the hills, while it again devastated every place below them, it outstripped all preventive measures … At last, after five days, an end was put to the conflagration … by the destruction of all buildings on a vast space, so that the violence of the fire was met by clear ground and an open sky. But before people laid aside their fears, the flames returned, with no less fury this second time … Rome, indeed, is divided into fourteen districts, four of which remained uninjured, three were leveled to the ground, while in the other seven were left only a few shattered, half-burnt relics of houses.

Fire was much more difficult to contain in ancient times than it is today. A fire could do incalculable damage before it was extinguished.

Crime and Punishment

Much like other facets of Roman society, criminals' punishments were handed down according to the social class of the criminal. Romans did not believe in jailing criminals long term. In fact, prison was a means of getting the accused to comply with magistrates. For convicted criminals, sentences ranged from forced labor to the death penalty. Upper-class criminals who were at risk of facing the death penalty were often allowed to go into permanent exile instead. Less severe crimes merited a temporary exile. The lower classes were not so lucky and paid a much harsher price for their crimes.

Aside from exile (and the death penalty), other punishments in the ancient empire included making financial restitution—the Roman government could seize assets and often did. Criminals also participated in gladiatorial games as a punishment. The term for gladiators who fought animals to make restitution for their crimes was *bestiarii*.

Some emperors made a name for themselves due to their cruel methods of exacting justice. Historically, Nero and Caligula stand out as two of the most blood thirsty.

Natural disasters also struck Roman cities from time to time. Early in the first century, the city of Sardis in Asia Minor was hit by a huge earthquake. The rebuilding of Sardis took more than a century. An earthquake that struck Pompeii in 62 CE did so much damage that some people thought this city should just be abandoned. It wasn't, and seventeen years later, Pompeii and the neighboring town of Herculaneum were the victims of one of history's most famous disasters, the eruption of Mount Vesuvius. Both cities were buried under deep layers of volcanic debris. The catastrophe, however, preserved the two towns in an almost untouched state. Since the eighteenth century, archaeologists have been carefully unearthing and studying them, revealing ever more information about urban life in the Roman Empire.

The ruins of Pompeii are a popular tourist destination.

EYEWITNESS TO VESUVIUS

Pliny the Elder, admiral and famous scholar, commanded the Roman fleet that was based about 19 miles (30 km) across the Bay of Naples from Pompeii. His seventeen-year-old nephew, Pliny the Younger, was visiting him when Vesuvius erupted. Later, Pliny the Younger wrote an eyewitness account of the disaster, beginning, "On 24 August, in the early afternoon, my mother drew his [Pliny the Elder's] attention to a cloud of unusual size … Its general appearance … [was] like an umbrella pine, for it rose to a great height on a sort of trunk and then split off into branches … Sometimes it looked white, sometimes blotched and dirty."

The admiral's scientific curiosity was awakened, and he set sail across the bay for a closer look. The expedition turned into a rescue mission, with several ships working to carry people away from the catastrophic eruption. "And now cinders, which grew thicker and hotter the nearer he approached, fell into the ships, then pumice stones, too, with stones blackened, scorched, and cracked by fire. Then the sea ebbed suddenly from under them, while the shore was blocked by landslips from the mountains."

Pliny the Elder commanded his ship to land about 4 miles (6.4 km) south of Pompeii. Unable to put to sea again because of fierce wind and waves, he took refuge for the night in a friend's villa. By early morning, "the courtyard giving access to his room was full of ashes mixed with pumice stones, so that its level had risen, and if he had stayed in the room any longer, he would never have got out. The buildings were now shaking with violent shocks, and seemed to be swaying to and fro, as if they were torn from their foundations." Back at the naval base, Pliny the Younger and his mother experienced these same tremors and fled their house:

The coaches that we had ordered out, though upon the most level ground, were sliding to and fro and could not be kept steady … Then we beheld the sea sucked back, leaving many sea animals captive on the dry sand … A black and dreadful cloud bursting out in gusts of igneous serpentine vapor now and again yawned open to reveal long, fantastic flames, resembling flashes of lightning but much larger. Soon afterward, the cloud began to descend upon the earth and cover the sea. Ashes now fell upon us, though as yet in no great quantity. I looked behind me; darkness came rolling over the land after us like a torrent. I proposed, while we yet could see, to turn aside, lest we should be knocked down in the road by a crowd that followed us, and trampled to death in the dark. We had scarce sat down when darkness overspread us … You could hear the shrieks of women and crying children and the shouts of men; some were seeking their children, others their parents; some praying to die, from the very fear of dying; many lifting their hands to the gods; but the greater part imagining that there were no gods left anywhere, that the last and eternal night was come upon the world.

This cloud of ash and poisonous gas thinned out as it crossed the bay, and so Pliny the Younger lived to tell the tale. His uncle was not so lucky. He had left the villa and gone to the shore to see if there was any way to escape. Surrounded by the dark cloud from the volcano, choking on the sulfurous fumes, Pliny the Elder collapsed on the beach and died, one of Vesuvius's thousands of victims.

GOVERNMENT AID

Emperors sent relief money and gave other assistance to cities hit by disaster. For example, after the earthquake in Sardis, the emperor Tiberius pledged a huge sum of money for rebuilding and canceled the Sardians' tax payments for five years. The emperor Titus arranged housing and financial help for many

Emperor Trajan began a welfare program to help children.

of the people who fled their homes when Vesuvius began to erupt. Other emperors, too, looked for various ways to improve life in the empire's cities.

For the city of Rome, Augustus established not only the police force–like urban cohort but also the *vigiles*. These were night watchmen and, more importantly, trained firefighters. There were 3,500 (later increased to 7,000) men in the vigiles, and some of them also did duty in Ostia, the port city that served Rome. The commander of the vigiles was an equestrian, but the firefighters themselves were freedmen.

The great fire of 64 CE showed that some blazes were too huge even for the vigiles to handle, so Nero decreed new fire safety regulations. These included limiting the height of apartment buildings, requiring fireproof stone to be used in a large part of all new construction, leaving more open space in front of buildings, and keeping firefighting equipment available in the courtyards of all residences. Many other cities followed Rome's model in setting up fire-safety laws and firefighting units.

Another urban problem that demanded attention was poverty. The patron-client relationship was a kind of welfare system, since patrons' gifts of food and money helped many of the working poor as well as the unemployed. But too often this was not enough. Many poor citizens relied on a monthly distribution of free grain by the government. The emperors did their best to help assure the timely delivery of large amounts of grain to Rome—there was always a danger of riots if the supply ran low. As an additional measure to keep the populace happy, emperors occasionally handed out gifts of money, food, and clothes.

In the second century CE, the emperor Trajan established a welfare program specifically to help poor children. Every year, a sum of money was distributed to various Italian cities for the benefit of these children. Many other wealthy Romans also set up charitable funds, like a man from North Africa who gave his city a large amount of money to take care of six hundred boys and girls. Among other charitable acts, Pliny the Younger donated funds to his hometown in northern Italy to support poor children and to establish a school, a library, and a bathhouse. Pliny and those like him felt that since they were fortunate enough to be wealthy and educated, it was their duty to use at least some of their resources for the public good.

This attitude toward charity and public service is one of the great legacies of the Roman Empire. Looking back, we may be able to learn from the Romans how to solve some of the problems that confront our cities and our society today. Sometimes the history of the empire shows us possible solutions; at other times it warns us what to avoid. The Romans laid much of the foundation for our modern city-based lifestyle. To know their story is to know ourselves all the better.

GLOSSARY

aedile

The magistrate responsible for the upkeep of buildings and city-wide festivals.

amphitheater

An oval, nearly circular stadium, mainly for shows involving combat or wild-animal fights.

aqueduct

An artificial channel to carry water from its source to a city.

arena

An amphitheater's central, ground-level area, where the spectacles took place.

atrium

The front room of a Roman house, used to receive visitors.

basilica

A large rectangular building used for public meetings, law courts, and government offices; in a private home, a basilica was a rectangular meeting room.

circus

A long, oval stadium where chariot races were held; a racetrack.

domus

A free-standing house.

duovir

A magistrate composed of two men.

equestrians

Members of Rome's second-highest class, ranking below senators; in general, they were wealthy businessmen.

eulogy

A speech given at a funeral to praise the dead person; upper-class Romans often delivered eulogies in the forum and then had them inscribed on marble.

forum

The civic center and main meeting place of a Roman city, with government buildings, offices, shops, and temples surrounding a large open area; in Rome itself there were six forums: the ancient original Forum, and additional forums built by Julius Caesar and by the emperors Augustus, Nerva, Vespasian, and Trajan.

fresco

A wall painting made on fresh plaster.

insula (plural **insulae**)

An apartment complex.

legion

A unit of the Roman army, made up of about five thousand men.

orator

A person skilled in writing and making speeches.

pantomime

A ballet-like performance in which dancers, accompanied by music, wordlessly acted out stories from myth or legend.

FURTHER INFORMATION

BOOKS

Biesty, Stephen. *Rome in Spectacular Cross-Section*. New York: ScholasticNonfiction, 2003.

Langley, Andrew. *The Roman News*. Cambridge, MA: Candlewick Press, 2009.

WEBSITES

Digital Augustan Rome
http://www.digitalaugustanrome.org
Navigate this interactive map to learn more about the city of Rome in 14 CE.

Romans: The City of Rome
http://www.bbc.co.uk/schools/primaryhistory/romans/city_of_rome
Find links, photos, videos, and fun facts on this website from the BBC.

10 Innovations That Built Ancient Rome
http://www.history.com/news/history-lists/10-innovations-that-built-ancient-rome
This website provides an in-depth look at the technological innovations that shaped the empire.

ORGANIZATIONS

The Classical Association of Canada
http://www.cac-scec.ca
The Classical Association of Canada (CAC) website is a wonderful resource. The organization is also home to two journals.

The Metropolitan Museum of Art
http://www.metmuseum.org/about-the-met/curatorial-departments/greek-and-roman-art
The Metropolitan Museum of Art is home to an impressive collection of Roman art; the curators maintain an online database of their collection.

SOURCE NOTES

Chapter 1: Cities Great and Small

p. 7, Livy. *The Early History of Rome: Books I–V.* Translated by Aubrey De Sélincourt. London: Penguin Books, 2002. p. 84

p. 8, Carcopino, Jerome. *Daily Life in Ancient Rome.* Edited by Henry T. Rowell. Translated by E. O. Lorimer. New Haven, CT: Yale University Press, 1968. p. 21

p. 10, Editors of Time-Life Books. *Rome: Echoes of Imperial Glory.* Alexandria, VA: Time-Life Books, 1994. p. 154

p. 10, Mellor, Ronald, ed. *The Historians of Ancient Rome: An Anthology of the Major Writings.* New York: Routledge, 1998. p. 404

p. 13, Dix, T. Keith. "'Public Libraries' in Ancient Rome: Ideology and Reality." *Libraries & Culture* 29, no. 3 (1994). p. 287

Chapter 2: The Urban Lifestyle

p. 15, Vitruvius. *The Ten Books on Architecture.* Translated by Morris Hicky Morgan. New York: Dover Publications, 1960. p. 21

p. 17, Grabsky, Phil. *I, Caesar: Ruling the Roman Empire.* London: BBC Books, 1997. p. 25

p. 20, Carcopino, Jerome. *Daily Life in Ancient Rome.* Edited by Henry T. Rowell. Translated by E. O. Lorimer. New Haven, CT: Yale University Press, 1968. p. 32

p. 22, Vitruvius. *The Ten Books on Architecture.* Translated by Morris Hicky Morgan. New York: Dover Publications, 1960. p. 14

Chapter 3: Hard at Work

p. 25, Livy. *The Early History of Rome: Books I-V.* Translated by Aubrey De Sélincourt. London: Penguin Books, 2002. p. 370

p. 27, Shelton, Jo-Ann. *As the Romans Did: A Source Book in Roman Social History.* 2nd ed. New York: Oxford University Press, 1998. p. 176

pp. 27–28, Ibid., pp. 182–183

p. 29, Wells, Colin. *The Roman Empire.* 2nd ed. Cambridge, MA: Harvard University Press, 1992. p. 41

p. 29, Boardman, John, et al., editors. *The Oxford Illustrated History of the Roman World.* Oxford: Oxford University Press, 1988. p. 341

p. 29, Shelton, Jo-Ann. *As the Romans Did: A Source Book in Roman Social History.* 2nd ed. New York: Oxford University Press, 1998. p. 195

Chapter 4: City Men

p. 33, Tacitus, Cornelius. *The Complete Works of Tacitus.* Edited by Moses Hadas. New York: Modern Library, 1942. p. 162

p. 35, Pliny. *Complete Letters.* Translated by P. G. Walsh. Oxford: Oxford University Press, 2006. p. 219

p. 37, Boardman, John, et al., editors. *The Oxford Illustrated History of the Roman World.* Oxford: Oxford University Press, 1988. p. 165

p. 38, Shelton, Jo-Ann. *As the Romans Did: A Source Book in Roman Social History.* 2nd ed. New York: Oxford University Press, 1998. p. 254

p. 39, Mellor, Ronald, ed. *The Historians of Ancient Rome: An Anthology of the Major Writings.* New York: Routledge, 1998. p. 446

Chapter 5: City Women

p. 41, Tacitus, Cornelius. *The Annals of Imperial Rome*. Translated by Michael Grant. London: Penguin Books, 1996. p. 52

p. 42, Shelton, Jo-Ann. *As the Romans Did: A Source Book in Roman Social History*. 2nd ed. New York: Oxford University Press, 1998. p. 299

p. 42, Fantham, Elaine, et al. *Women in the Classical World: Image and Text*. New York: Oxford University Press, 1994. p. 318

p. 44, Adkins, Lesley, and Roy Adkins. *Handbook to Life in Ancient Rome*. New York, NY: Facts on File, 1994. p. 340

p. 45, Fantham, Elaine, et al. *Women in the Classical World: Image and Text*. New York: Oxford University Press, 1994. p. 368

Chapter 6: Childhood in the City

p. 47, Tertullian. *Christian and Pagan in the Roman Empire: The Witness of Tertullian*. Edited by Robert D. Sider. Washington, DC: Catholic University of America Press, 2001.

p. 48, Shelton, Jo-Ann. *As the Romans Did: A Source Book in Roman Social History*. 2nd ed. New York: Oxford University Press, 1998. p. 28

p. 50, Ibid., p. 102

p. 52, Fantham, Elaine, et al. *Women in the Classical World: Image and Text*. New York: Oxford University Press, 1994. p. 377

Chapter 7: Leisure Pursuits

p. 55, Tacitus, Cornelius. *The Complete Works of Tacitus*. Edited by Moses Hadas. New York: Modern Library, 1942. p. 758

p. 57, Shelton, Jo-Ann. *As the Romans Did: A Source Book in Roman Social History*. 2nd ed. New York: Oxford University Press, 1998. p. 319

p. 57, Carcopino, Jerome. *Daily Life in Ancient Rome*. Edited by Henry T. Rowell. Translated by E. O. Lorimer. New Haven, CT: Yale University Press, 1968. p. 227

p. 60, Scarre, Chris. *Chronicle of the Roman Emperors: The Reign-by-Reign Record of the Rulers of Imperial Rome*. London: Thames & Hudson, 1995. p. 73

p. 60, Shelton, Jo-Ann. *As the Romans Did: A Source Book in Roman Social History*. 2nd ed. New York: Oxford University Press, 1998. p. 355

Chapter 8: Crime and Danger

p. 63, Seneca, Lucius Annaeus. *Six Tragedies*. Translated by Emily R. Wilson. Oxford: Oxford University Press, 2010. p. 149

p. 64, Vitruvius. *The Ten Books on Architecture*. Translated by Morris Hicky Morgan. New York: Dover Publications, 1960. p. 247

p. 65, Mellor, Ronald, ed. *The Historians of Ancient Rome: An Anthology of the Major Writings*. New York: Routledge, 1998. pp. 471–472

p. 67, Wells, Colin. *The Roman Empire*. 2nd ed. Cambridge, MA: Harvard University Press, 1992. p. 188

p. 68, Editors of Time-Life Books. *Pompeii: The Vanished City*. Alexandria, VA: Time-Life Books, 1992. p. 23

pp. 68–69, Shelton, Jo-Ann. *As the Romans Did: A Source Book in Roman Social History*. 2nd ed. New York: Oxford University Press, 1998. p. 36

BIBLIOGRAPHY

Adkins, Lesley, and Roy A. Adkins. *Handbook to Life in Ancient Rome.* New York: Oxford University Press, 1994.

Boardman, John, et al., eds. *The Oxford Illustrated History of the Roman World.* Oxford: Oxford University Press, 1988.

Carcopino, Jerome. *Daily Life in Ancient Rome.* Edited by Henry T. Rowell. Translated by E. O. Lorimer. New Haven, CT: Yale University Press, 1968.

Dix, T. Keith. "'Public Libraries' in Ancient Rome: Ideology and Reality." *Libraries & Culture* 29, no. 3 (1994): 282–96.

Editors of Time-Life Books. *Pompeii: The Vanished City.* Alexandria, VA: Time-Life Books, 1992.

———. *Rome: Echoes of Imperial Glory.* Alexandria, VA: Time-Life Books, 1994.

Fantham, Elaine, et al. *Women in the Classical World: Image and Text.* New York: Oxford University Press, 1994.

Highet, Gilbert. *Poets in a Landscape.* New York: Alfred A. Knopf, 1957.

Mellor, Ronald, ed. *The Historians of Ancient Rome: An Anthology of the Major Writings.* New York: Routledge, 1998.

Scarre, Chris. *Chronicle of the Roman Emperors: The Reign-by-Reign Record of the Rulers of Imperial Rome.* London: Thames & Hudson, 1995.

Shelton, Jo-Ann. *As the Romans Did: A Source Book in Roman Social History.* 2nd ed. New York: Oxford University Press, 1998.

Vitruvius. *The Ten Books on Architecture.* Translated by Morris Hicky Morgan. New York: Dover Publications, 1960.

Wells, Colin. *The Roman Empire.* 2nd ed. Cambridge, MA: Harvard University Press, 1992.

INDEX

Page numbers in **boldface** are illustrations. Entries in **boldface** are glossary terms.